Introduction

Llanidloes rightly lays claim to be the 'first to
longest river, which takes its rise on the ri
9 miles to the west of the town. The town grew up around the ~~~~~~~~~~~
church founded by St Idloes, receiving a Royal Charter in 1282 enabling it to
hold fairs and a weekly market. It became a self-governing borough in 1344; a
status retained until 1974.

Llanidloes, or simply *Llani* to the locals, once had thriving wool, lead
mining and flannel industries, all making use of freely available water-power
from the rivers Severn and Clywedog. These industries fell into decline
over the years and all that now remains are some rather picturesque ruins
or tastefully restored factory buildings converted to residential use. Whilst
no longer buzzing with the various industries of times past, Llanidloes still
retains a vibrancy and life of its own. There is a keen spirit of regeneration
and a sense of looking to the future. Llanidloes welcomes visitors and not for
nothing is it known as 'the friendly town'.

The River Severn, or to give it its Welsh name, Afon Hafren, together with
the Clywedog, have long formed the life-blood of the town and, these days,
are central to an extensive network of footpaths and bridleways that take in
some of the most beautiful views in Mid Wales. Llanidloes town has a wealth
of historical buildings including the Old Market Hall, built in about 1600 and
standing at the intersection of the town's four main streets. It has served a
variety of purposes in its time and now houses an exhibition of timber-framed
buildings.

Other attractions in the area are Llyn Clywedog, which has the tallest
mass concrete dam in the UK; the Bryntail lead mine ruins; the Severn Way;
the Wye Valley Walk; Glyndŵr's Way National Trail; the Hafren Forest and
the upland wilderness of the five peaks of Plynlimon, the highest points in
the central range of the Cambrian Mountains. The area is an ideal spot for
those wishing to walk in outstanding scenery with a diverse range of wildlife
to observe. Llanidloes and the surrounding area has an excellent range of
accommodation available, which can be found through the local website,
www.llanidloes.com.

The walks in this book vary in length from about 3 to 10½ miles and
cover a variety of terrains, from open fields to lake-side, from moorland to
forest. Most are well within the capabilities of anyone with an average fitness
level and all have been chosen to give a flavour of this lovely yet largely
undiscovered part of Mid-Wales. But be warned, sample just one or two of our
walks and, like many others, you will find yourself drawn to returning again
and again to savour the 'Llanidloes Experience'.

WALK I

ALLT GOCH

DESCRIPTION A short walk of about 2½ miles through Allt Goch wood. The going is good under foot and the climbs are reasonable, with rest benches at intervals.
START Old Market Hall, Llanidloes, (SN 954846).

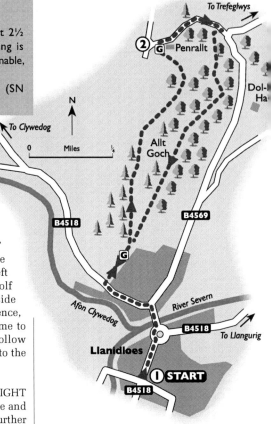

From the Old Market Hall, walk along Long Bridge Street to the roundabout and turn LEFT over the bridge. Turn LEFT again along the B4518 signposted to Llyn Clywedog and, after about 200 yards, Turn RIGHT off the road at the finger post for Glyndŵr's Way and the Severn Way. After going through the kissing gate, bear immediately LEFT up the hill and continue AHEAD up the hill, ignoring any paths crossing from left to right. On reaching the stile into the golf club, do not cross it, but turn RIGHT inside the fence and continue parallel to the fence, staying on the upper path until you come to the way marker for Glyndŵr's Way. Follow the way marks onto the golf course and to the clubhouse.

2 On reaching the clubhouse, bear RIGHT and leave the course through the gate and over the cattle grid and, ignoring any further way marks for Glyndŵr's Way, follow the tarmac road down to its junction with the Llanidloes/Trefeglwys road. Before reaching the road, turn RIGHT along the footpath climbing up into Allt Goch wood once again, turn LEFT near the top and follow the path down through the wood to its junction with the Severn Way at the car park. Turn RIGHT along the Severn Way and, on reaching the B4518, Turn LEFT and retrace your route through Llanidloes back to your start point.

WALK 2

ALLT GOCH AND THE SEVERN WAY

DESCRIPTION A longer walk of some 4½ miles through woodland, then along the Severn Way for a stretch before returning to Llanidloes along a quiet tarmac road.
START Old Market Hall, Llanidloes, (SN 954846).

From the Old Market Hall, walk along Long Bridge Street to the roundabout and

2

turn LEFT over the bridge. Turn LEFT again along the B4518 signposted to Llyn Clwedog. After about 200 yards, turn RIGHT at the finger post for Glyndŵr's Way and the Severn Way. Go AHEAD through the kissing gate and then bear LEFT, up through the wood at the point where Glyndŵr's Way leaves the Severn Way. Follow the way marks for Glyndŵr's Way to the golf course and bear right in front of the club-house, leaving the course via the gate and cattle grid onto the tarmac road.

2 After about 50 yards turn LEFT off the road, following the way marks for Glyndŵr's Way and go through the farm gate AHEAD of you. Follow the track and stay on it past the point where Glyndŵr's Way leaves the track to your left. Continue AHEAD through two gates and then follow the track through fields as it curves away to the right, through another gate and then down to the Llanidloes/Trefeglwys road. Cross the road

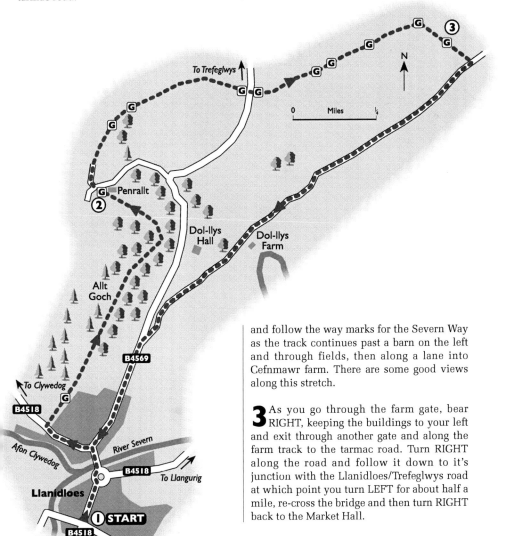

and follow the way marks for the Severn Way as the track continues past a barn on the left and through fields, then along a lane into Cefnmawr farm. There are some good views along this stretch.

3 As you go through the farm gate, bear RIGHT, keeping the buildings to your left and exit through another gate and along the farm track to the tarmac road. Turn RIGHT along the road and follow it down to it's junction with the Llanidloes/Trefeglwys road at which point you turn LEFT for about half a mile, re-cross the bridge and then turn RIGHT back to the Market Hall.

WALK 3
ALLT GOCH, CROES LLWYN & THE SEVERN WAY

DESCRIPTION An extension of **Walk 2** covering about 6½ miles including sections of woodland, fields and tarmac road.
START Old Market Hall, Llanidloes, (SN 954846).

I Leave the Old Market Hall along Long Bridge Street and turn LEFT at the roundabout and on over the Severn Bridge. Turn LEFT immediately along the road signposted to Llyn Clywedog and continue for about 200 yards until you reach the finger post directing you off RIGHT along Glyndŵr's Way and the Severn Way. Continue along the trail through Allt Goch wood until you reach the point where Glyndŵr's Way bears off to the LEFT and follow the way marks until you reach the golf clubhouse. Turn RIGHT along the tarmac drive and over the cattle grid for about 50 yards where you will follow the marked trail to the LEFT along a drive through a farm. Walk AHEAD, up the lane and look out for the way mark post on your right indicating that Glyndŵr's Way leaves the bridleway at that point, and take the stile to your LEFT. Follow the way marks down over two more stiles and, at the second of these, bear diagonally RIGHT down the field and exit via a field gate onto the road.

2 Turn RIGHT along the road along which, to your left, you may see extensive views of Y Fan hamlet, once the site of extensive lead mining, but now cleared and landscaped. Continue along the road for about half a mile, past a bridleway coming in from your left, and on to Hiriaeth farm. Just past the farm, go through the gate facing you on the RIGHT hand side of the road and follow the track for about 150 yards, past a water trough and then go through the field gate on your RIGHT. The track is easy to follow up the hill, through the fields to the tarmac road above.

3 On reaching the road, cross over and walk AHEAD and slightly to your left, along the farm track marked 'No through road' to Croesllwyn farm. Bear LEFT through the farm and exit through the gate. The track curves down to your right and, where it forks, take the RIGHT fork down to the small pool on your right. Just past the pool, go through the way marked gate on your RIGHT and walk diagonally LEFT up the field to the gate in the top corner. Follow the way marks up the hill, keeping the fence to your right and, at the end of the fence, bear RIGHT and go through the gate into Dol Llys Fach, past the house and out along the drive to the tarmac road.

4 Turn RIGHT along the road for about 250 yards and then turn RIGHT along the way marked farm track to Cefnmawr. On reaching the buildings, follow the track as it goes through a gate to your LEFT around the outside of the buildings before exiting LEFT again through another gate. The track is then easy to follow through the fields, past a barn on your right and out to the tarmac road. Cross the road and go through the gateway AHEAD, continuing to follow the track as it passes through one gate then a set of two, before continuing AHEAD down the lane to Penrallt. On reaching the tarmac road, turn RIGHT to the golf course and after crossing the cattle grid, turn LEFT and follow the way marks for Glyndŵr's Way down through Allt Goch woods to the B4518, where you turn LEFT to go down to the junction, turn RIGHT over the bridge to the roundabout and, turning RIGHT again, retrace your route back to the Market Hall.

4

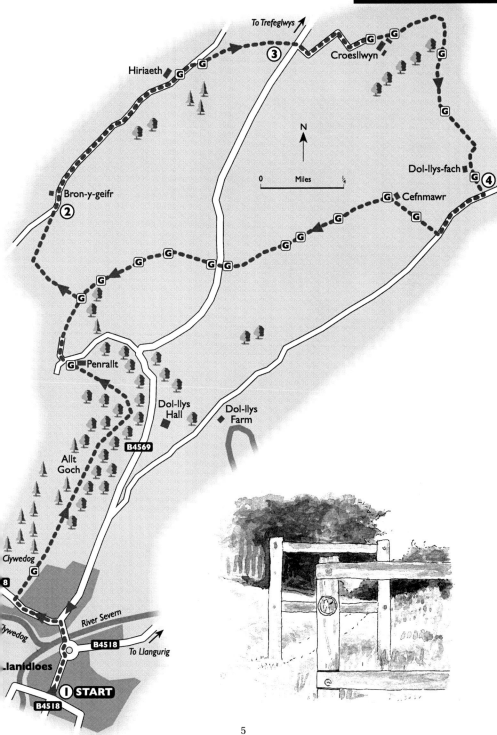

To Trefeglwys

③

Croesllwyn

Hiriaeth

Dol-llys-fach

④

Bron-y-geifr

②

Cefnmawr

N

0 Miles ¼

Penrallt

Dol-llys
Hall

Dol-llys
Farm

B4569

Allt
Goch

Clywedog

8

River Severn

Clywedog

B4518

To Llangurig

.lanidloes

① START

B4518

5

CAENCOED, CEFNBEIDIOG & THE SEVERN VALLEY

DESCRIPTION A fairly gentle walk of about 3 miles, with one steep climb up the field after the first stile, having excellent views over Llanidloes and of the upper Severn Valley.

START Old Market Hall, Llanidloes, (SN 954846).

the next stile is somewhat hidden by the fall of the slope to the trees. Climb the stile into the wood and follow the track, keeping the hedge to your left, until you emerge onto Caencoed farm rear drive, then turn RIGHT onto the tarmac road.

2 Turn RIGHT along the road until it becomes an un-surfaced track. *There are good views here over the upper Severn Valley.* Continue AHEAD, through Cefnbeidiog to Belan. At Belan, go straight AHEAD through the yard, keeping all buildings to your right, and then turn RIGHT behind the buildings, following the bridleway down to the tarmac road. Turn RIGHT along the road, signed

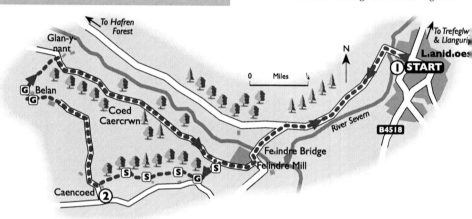

I From the Old Market Hall, walk along Short Bridge Street and cross the Severn bridge. Turn LEFT along Penygreen Road and walk for about half a mile until you reach the turning signposted to Llangurig. Turn LEFT here, down over Felindre bridge and, ignoring the right turn into the housing estate, take the first turn RIGHT, following the sign for the Severn Way. After about 200 yards, past a barn conversion, turn LEFT up some steps over a stile and follow the way marks up the hill and through a gate into the next field. *As you walk up the hill, looking back down the valley provides particularly good views over Llanidloes.* After crossing another stile, keeping the fence line to your left, go through a gate and then bear diagonally RIGHT over the field to the far corner where

the Severn Way and follow it back into Llanidloes and your start point.

From industry to idyll

Walk through the rural landscape of the valleys of the Clywedog and Severn today and there is an air of timelessness about it. It can be difficult to imagine that in the mid-19th and early 20th centuries these very rivers provided the lifeblood of a thriving industrial town, and that along their banks sprang factories and mills for the processing of corn, wool leather and iron.

Water power provided the energy to drive the machinery that took hitherto cottage activities and catapulted them into the industrial age. Carding mills, spinning and weaving shops and fulling mills grew and employed vast numbers of workers, many of whom moved into the area from elsewhere. A thriving flannel industry and the coming of the railway made Welsh flannel a renowned commodity.

Lead mining had taken had taken place in various parts of the area since the 17th century, with small mines opening and closing as seams were discovered and exhausted, with the most productive at the time being the Bryntail and Penclun mines. However the discovery of the rich Cwm Phillip vein in 1865 led to the opening of the Van mine, soon to become one of the greatest mines in Britain. Again water and water power were essential elements for the mining and processing of lead ore.

Competition from the Yorkshire woollen industry, undercapitalisation and a slowness to modernise all contributed to the decline of the wool-based industries in the early 20th century. Productivity of the lead mines declined, closures occurred and by the 1920s many miners and left for the South Wales coal pits. Remains of the mines can be seen at Bryntail, Penclun and Y Fan.

Some factory buildings remain within the town and have been successfully converted to other uses – note the Bridgend Flannel Mill, now an apartment building, on Short Bridge. Near the start of **Walk 4**, at Felindre Bridge on the far side of the small housing estate, you may still see the Felindre Corn Mill, now a private house. The last traces of Caen Coed Mill, where fulling, carding, spinning and weaving were carried out, have all but disappeared and are now overgrown.

Enjoy this short walk but do pause for a while and try to imagine what was a very different landscape a hundred years ago.

Caencoed Factory *(centre left, above)*, on the Upper Severn near Glan y nant, was built by Mr. Stephens in 1809 and later worked by Richard Brown and his son Owen Brown. In September 1880 the Montgomeryshire Express reported an improvement in the flannel industry and stated machinery was to be set up at Caencoed (and Glan Clywedog) which had been shut for many years. In the early part of this century the factory passed to Richard Owen of Glan y nant. It was destroyed by fire in 1923. Notice the tenter frames (racks or deintir) on the hillside in the right foreground.

Another well known factory a little further up river was the Nantyrhebog (Alba or Herberts), first built in 1797. Unfortunately, no photo of this building has been found.

Felindre Corn Mill

CLYWEDOG, BRYNTAIL AND PENCLUN

DESCRIPTION A gem of a walk of about 4½ miles taking in Llyn Clywedog and its dams, the Bryntail mines and a pretty valley walk around Penclun.

START Bryntail car park, Clywedog, (SN 914868).

DIRECTIONS Leave Llanidloes along the B4518 signposted for Llyn Clywedog for about 3½ miles and then take the left turn, again signposted for Llyn Clywedog for a further 1½ miles and then turn right at the sign for the Bryntail Mines. Park in the car park.

I From the car park, follow the way marks for Glyndŵr's Way into the Bryntail site and pause for a while to explore the ruins of the old lead mines. Then follow the way marks for Glyndŵr's Way up the hill as the well-marked path leaves the site near the information board. At the top of the hill, bear LEFT and continue to follow the way marks to Bryntail Farm. At the farm go straight AHEAD and out along the farm track to the tarmac road.

2 Cross the road and go AHEAD through the farm gate signed for Penclun and along the track. As you walk along the track, you will have excellent views of Y Fan hamlet to your right. On reaching Penclun, go through the gate and follow the track to the right and then bear LEFT below the farm buildings. *At this point, if you look down to your right, just below the track, you may see the remains of the old pumping house for the, now long gone, Penclun Lead Mines.* Go through two further gates and continue along the track for about 150 yards or so. Where it

appears to fork, take the upper option to your LEFT and go through the gate. The track continues around the side of the hill as it opens into a picturesque valley. Across the valley to your right you may spot a ruined house and, below it, the remains of an early dam, built to provide power for the Van lead mines further down the valley. The dam failed many years ago and has since been made safe. As you descend and join a more substantial track along the valley floor, look out for the way marker at which you turn RIGHT off the track and onto a bridleway. Follow the bridleway and cross a stream after which the trail becomes difficult to spot in places, but keeping the stream to your left will provide a sufficient guide until you reach a more substantial bridleway crossing from right to left. *At this point, if you are feeling particularly energetic, you may turn right and follow the easily visible green trail to the trig point on the top of Bryn y Fan from which there are stunning views of Llyn Clywedog.* Turn LEFT here and follow the track out through the gate and turn RIGHT up to the Bwlch y Gle dam and then LEFT along the road to the car park. There are toilets here.

3 Leave the car park and turn LEFT along the road and up the hill for about a quarter of a mile. Go through the field gate on your RIGHT and then bear diagonally LEFT to a further field gate in the hedge crossing in front of you. Go through this gate and, keeping the fence line to your left, continue along the trail, passing a stand of trees on your right, and follow the trail on down the hill back into Bryntail Farm. In the yard, turn RIGHT to the farm gate you originally entered by and follow the way marks for Glyndŵr's Way back down to the Bryntail Mines. *On leaving the car park it is well worth turning right along the road to the Llyn Clywedog viewpoint from where there are excellent views of the lake, dam and mines.* From here simply follow the road back to Llanidloes and your start point.

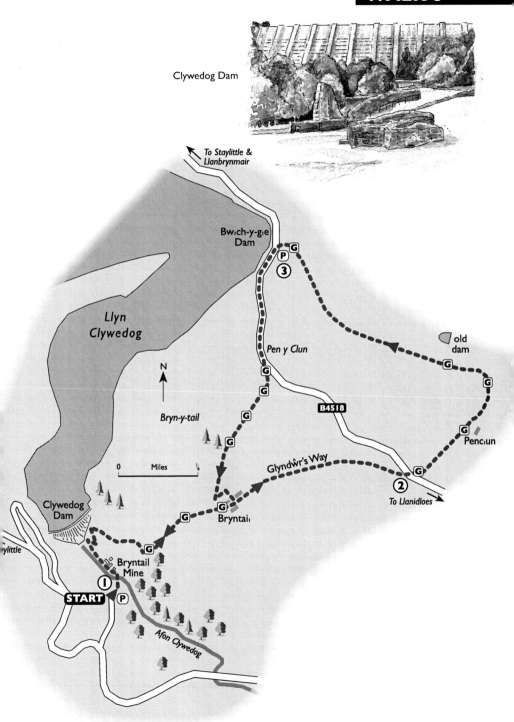

Clywedog Dam

To Staylittle & Llanbrynmair

Bwlch-y-gle Dam

Llyn Clywedog

Pen y Clun

old dam

N

Bryn-y-tail

B4518

Penciun

0   Miles   ¼

Glyndŵr's Way

Clywedog Dam

Bryntail

To Llanidloes

ylittle

Bryntail Mine

START

Afon Clywedog

9

WALK 6
GLYNDŴR'S WAY
&
THE CLYWEDOG VALLEY

DESCRIPTION A walk of approximately 6 miles, the first half along Glyndŵr's Way with extensive views from Garth Hill over to Bryn y Fan and the old lead mine workings at Van, and returning along the picturesque Clywedog valley back to the Market Hall.
START Old Market Hall, Llanidloes, (SN 954846).

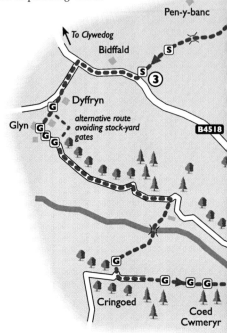

I Leave the Old Market Hall along Long Bridge Street and turn LEFT at the roundabout and on over the Severn bridge. Turn LEFT immediately along the road signposted to Llyn Clywedog and continue for about 200 yards until you reach the finger post directing you off RIGHT along Glyndŵr's Way and the Severn Way. Continue along the trail through Allt Goch wood until you reach the point where Glyndŵr's Way bears off to the LEFT and follow the way marks until you reach the golf clubhouse. Turn RIGHT along the tarmac drive and over the cattle grid for about 50 yards where you will follow the marked trail to the LEFT along a drive through a farm. Walk AHEAD, up the lane and look out for the way mark post on your right indicating that Glyndŵr's Way leaves the bridleway at that point, and take the stile to your LEFT. Follow the way marks down over two more stiles and, at the second of these, bear diagonally RIGHT down the field and exit via a field gate onto the road.

2 Turn RIGHT along the road and, after about 25 yards, again pick up the way mark for Glyndŵr's Way and bear LEFT over the stile. Follow the way marks down the fields over two further stiles, and leave the fields through the gate onto the Van road. Walk AHEAD straight over the road and along the drive towards Garth farm but don't

miss the way mark taking you off the drive to your RIGHT, up through a small patch of woodland. As you follow the well-defined track along the fence line, you will see expanding views

over the hamlet of Van and the old lead mines. The trail rises up to a fence with a gate and stile by a small quarry. Cross the stile and emerge into open fields through which the trail continues AHEAD as a green track, below and to the right of the top of Garth Hill. Go through the LEFT hand of the two gates ahead of you where the trail continues along a narrow lane. On exiting the lane through a gate, follow the marked trail sharp LEFT, then sharp RIGHT when it meets the fence. Keeping the fence to your left, cross over a small footbridge next to a stile and then go through the gate next to another stile. As the trail reaches the drive to Pen y Banc farm, go over the stile to your LEFT, into the field and walk along the fence parallel to the drive until you exit over a further stile onto the tarmac road.

through the farm buildings and, on reaching the 'L' shaped building in front of you, turn LEFT and leave the farm through the gate AHEAD and, after passing through a further two gates, reach and continue along the tarmac road. The road slopes down through Brithdir wood with the Clywedog river down to your right. After about 600 yards, the road takes a sharp hairpin turn to the left then right. About 200 yards further on, it does the same, but immediately before this second 'kink' follow the track off to your RIGHT, down the hill with a stream on your left. Continue down past some buildings to your left to the river Clywedog where, turning to your RIGHT, you cross the old iron footbridge over the river. Climb out the other side, through a gate to meet a well-established track joining you down hill from your right. Turn LEFT along this track and, where the track bears off to the left, go through the field gate immediately AHEAD of you. Keeping the tree line to your right, continue along the top of the field, through two further gateways and, after crossing a small stream (sometimes dry in the Summer), go through the gate into the forestry plantation. Keeping the edge of the wood to your right, follow the track until you emerge onto a grassy track and follow it with a caravan site to your left, over the river Clywedog. When the track meets a gateway to a bungalow, take the short path down to your left, over the stile, and continue down through an old kissing gate, over a small footbridge and climb up the field to the stone track along the forestry fence line. Turn left along this track and follow it through a gate until it meets the tarmac road, which you follow back down into Llanidloes, crossing the bridge over the Severn and back to your start point.

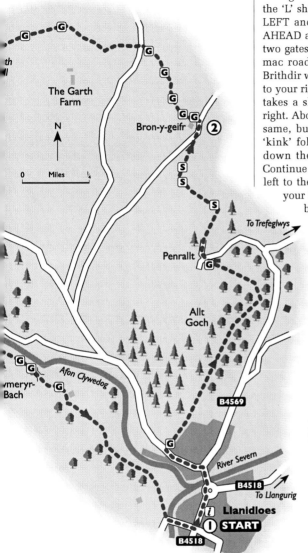

The Garth Farm

N

0   Miles   ¼

Bron-y-geifr   ②

To Trefeglwys

Penrallt

Allt Goch

Afon Clywedog

meryr-Bach

B4569

River Severn

B4518

To Llangurig

Llanidloes

START

B4518

3 Turn RIGHT along the road for about 250 yards, then turn LEFT towards Llyn Clywedog and, after a further 200 yards or so, turn off LEFT along the drive to Dyffryn. Walk

MARSH'S POOL (LLYN GLYNBROCHAN)

DESCRIPTION A particularly scenic walk of about 6½ miles offering superb views over Llanidloes itself and a pause at the beautiful Marsh's Pool.

START Old Market Hall, Llanidloes, (SN 954846).

I From the Old Market Hall walk along Short Bridge Street and, after crossing the Severn Bridge, turn LEFT along Penygreen Road. After about half a mile, turn LEFT down the single track road signposted to Llangurig and drop down over Felindre Bridge. Ignore the two right turns and continue to where the road itself bears sharply right. At this point you will see a finger post indicating a bridleway through a field gate AHEAD of you, next to a bungalow. Go through the gate and walk down the field, keeping the hedge to your left until you reach the river, where you bear RIGHT until you reach the river bridge on your LEFT.

2 Cross the bridge and walk up the narrow lane and through the gate at the end. On leaving the lane, head diagonally RIGHT to the top of the field, keeping just to the left of the lone telegraph pole in the middle. Looking back from this point will provide excellent views over Llanidloes and its surrounds. Go through the gate at the top corner and follow the track AHEAD, up through the wood then alongside open fields to Cefn y Bwlch farm. At this point you will have to follow the way marks around to the left of the buildings before rejoining the track as it climbs the hill. After climbing up the track and emerging onto open fields, follow the bridleway down the hill and, keeping the hedge to your right, note a gateway marked with a 'footpath' sign on your right. (*You will return to this point later*).

3 Continue down and through a short wooded area that can be quite wet and muddy after rain, and emerge through a gate into a more open, but scrubby, area. Keeping the fence line to your right, skirt around a patch of gorse and then walk AHEAD through a gate into a conifer plantation. After about 250 yards, the path joins a more distinct track coming in from your left. Continue AHEAD but note this point for your return journey as it is possible to miss the junction coming the other way. On emerging from the woods, continue AHEAD down the hill, keeping the fence to your right, where you will soon see Marsh's Pool through the trees. *The pool and surrounding area are private, but a glance at the map will show the footpaths and bridleways around the pool, some of which offer excellent photographic opportunities.*

4 After enjoying the pool and it's surrounds, return through the conifer plantation and up the hill to point **3** and turn LEFT through the gate along the footpath through the fields and down to The Farm where, on entering the farmyard, you turn LEFT across the front of the house and go through the gate AHEAD of you and out into the field. Follow the footpath down the hill, past the ruined cottage (Ty'n y Coed) in the trees, and along to the small bridge crossing the Afon Brochan. After crossing, continue AHEAD, up the slope and through the gates to the tarmac road where you turn RIGHT and return to Llanidloes and your start point.

12

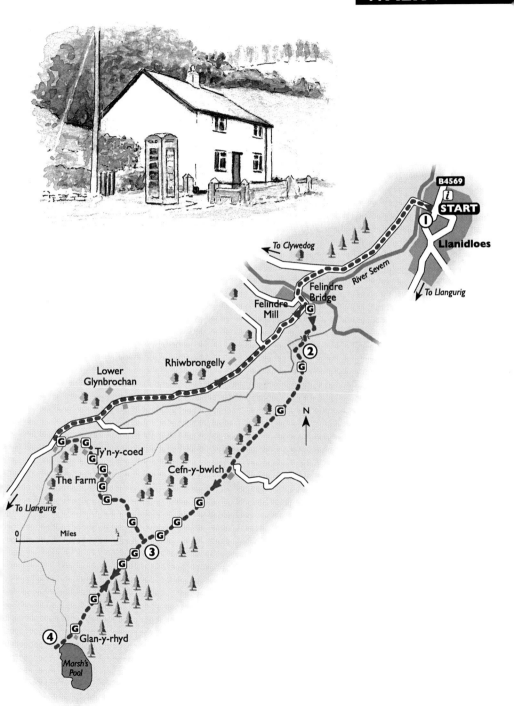

NANT Y GEIFR & THE SEVERN VALLEY

DESCRIPTION A walk of about 6½ miles, just over half being along minor roads, that allows access to one of Llanidloes' jewels, the Nant y Geifr reservoir. There are no steep climbs although some of the going may be a little rough under foot.

START Old Market Hall, Llanidloes, (SN 954846).

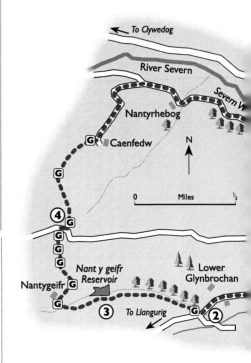

From the Old Market Hall, walk along Short Bridge Street and, crossing the Severn Bridge, turn LEFT along Penygreen Road. After about half a mile, turn LEFT down the minor road signposted to Llangurig and, ignoring the two right turns, follow the road as it bears sharp right and continue up the hill for about a mile. After passing Rhiwbrongelly and Lower Glynbrochan farms you will come to a house and barns with an old, red telephone box on your right.

2 At the end of the last building on your right, turn RIGHT through the gate and walk up the bank towards the old ruined chapel, passing between it and the hedge on your left. Continue AHEAD through the trees, keeping the hedge to your left until you emerge over a stile into an open field. Carry on walking straight AHEAD and, after passing through into a larger field, walk along the slope keeping just above the mid line between the hedges to your left and right. Go through the gate into the next field and keep close to the fence on your right. After a few yards you will come to a stile in the fence. Climb over the stile and down the steps onto the Nant y Geifr dam and spend a few minutes enjoying this very pretty spot. Although there is generally no public access to the reservoir, Severn Trent Water have kindly permitted installation of the stile and seats to allow walkers to visit and enjoy the view. In the spring the rhododendrons are spectacular. *The Severn Trent ask that you do not venture onto the causeway to the valve platform as it is not maintained for public safety and could prove dangerous.*

3 To leave the reservoir, climb back over the stile, turn RIGHT and resume walking along your original route, keeping the fence to your right, until the field broadens and you will see where the lower flat area ahead of you has been cultivated. This area can be very soft and muddy and you should, at this point, keep to it's outside edge, along the bottom of the slope until you are able to come back in to meet the fence once more in the corner of the field. On meeting the fence you will come to a wicket gate. Go through the gate and cross the stream. After crossing the stream, bear diagonally LEFT up the field and go through the gate into the award winning Nant y Geifr farm. Bear RIGHT through the farm and exit along the drive AHEAD of you until you come to the footpath sign on a field gate on your LEFT. Go through the gate and, keeping the fence to your left, follow the footpath to the tarmac road. (*At this point you may shorten your route by about a mile by turning RIGHT and following the road to the 'T' junction, where you bear LEFT and continue back to your starting point*).

4 Turn RIGHT along the road then, after about 75 yards, turn LEFT along the bridleway, keeping the fence to your right as you go down hill. This section offers pleasant vistas over the Severn Valley. The bridleway then passes through a gate into a lane taking you to Caenfedw where you turn LEFT along the unclassified road down to it's junction with the Severn Way. Turn RIGHT along the Severn Way and, enjoying the views over the upper Severn Valley, follow the road back to Llanidloes and your start point.

B4569

START

Llanidloes

River Severn

To Llangurig

Felindre Bridge

Felindre Mill

hiwbrongelly

LLANDINAM TO HORNBY, RHYD FAES AND RETURN

DESCRIPTION A 6 mile walk along some tarmac road, bridleway and the Severn Way with views over the Severn valley and the village of Llandinam to the Llandinam Wind Farm. The route has no real climbs but does involve a fairly steep descent for about 200 yards near the end.
START Public car park next to the Lion Hotel, (SO 026884).
DIRECTIONS From Llanidloes take the A470 North for about 6 miles until you reach the village of Llandinam. The public car park is on the left just before the Lion Hotel.

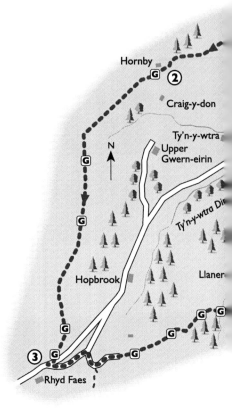

I Turn LEFT out of the car park and walk along the footpath past the Lion and turn LEFT over the iron bridge crossing the river Severn by the statue of David Davies. Continue for about 300 yards when the road will bear sharp RIGHT and, after a further 300 yards, look out for the finger post on your right and a post box on your left. At this point turn LEFT up through the houses until, at the end of the road, you meet a stile on your RIGHT. After crossing the stile walk straight over the field to the next stile *(*)* where you emerge onto a tarmac road and pass through the field gate on the opposite side. Walk out onto the field and, after bearing RIGHT to pass through the gap in the hedge, walk to the far LEFT hand corner of the field and climb over the stile onto the tarmac road. Turn LEFT along the road and after about 200 yards, turn RIGHT at the junction signposted for Caersws and Trefeglwys. Continue along this road, passing a farm entrance on your left and follow it up the hill as it swings to the left. Turn LEFT into the second farm lane entrance, over a cattle grid, and walk along the lane to Hornby Farm.

2 Follow the bridleway straight through Hornby and, after passing through the farm gate, walk on along a short lane and out on to open fields. *As you walk along the bridleway, if you look to your left you will see part of the Llandinam wind farm and, looking to your right, the wind turbines at Carno.* Follow the bridleway until it reaches the tarmac road at Rhyd Faes.

3 At this point turn RIGHT along the road and then immediately LEFT, following the road down the hill to the 'T' junction where you turn RIGHT by Maes Derw bungalow. About 100 yards farther along the road, you will see the waymarks for the Severn Way. Turn LEFT along the Way, following the way marks until you reach the point where the trail crosses a stream near some sheep pens. At this point, you bear diagonally LEFT

16

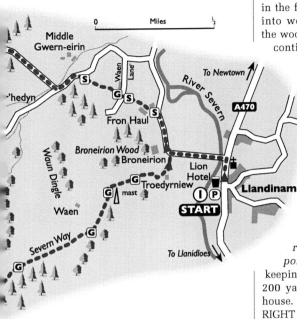

over the field until you cross a small stream in the far corner and go through a field gate into woodland. Follow the track through the wood until you exit into open fields and continue, keeping the fence to your left until you pass through a gate where a track crosses your front from right to left, part of the Severn Way. Turn LEFT along the track until you reach the radio mast and then turn RIGHT through the wicket gate next to it. (*If you wish to avoid the steep descent, carry straight on past the mast until you join the tarmac road and then turn RIGHT over the stile (*) you crossed on the way out and, after crossing the field and leaving the houses, turn RIGHT along the road and continue back to your start point*). Descend the fairly steep slope, keeping the fence line to your left, for about 200 yards until you reach Troed Y Rhiw house. Turn LEFT along the drive and then RIGHT at the end to take you back over the iron bridge and RIGHT to return to your start point.

David Davies
of Llandinam,
dock and railway
builder

LLANDINAM AND MOEL IART

DESCRIPTION An interesting and picturesque walk of about 6½ miles through the village of Llandinam and then along bridleways around Moel Iart hill, offering views over the Severn valley on one side and over the Mochdre valley on the other side. The route involves a moderate climb and a short stretch across scrubby upland.

START Public car park next to the Lion Hotel, Llandinam, (SO 026884).

DIRECTIONS From Llanidloes, take the A470 North for about 6 miles until you reach the village of Llandinam. The public car park is on the left just before the Lion Hotel.

I Leaving the car park, turn LEFT along the A470 and cross the road opposite the village post office. Turn RIGHT into the village and, ignoring the two left turnings, continue AHEAD, up the hill and out of the village. After just over ½ mile, you will come to a right turn called Cobbler's Corner, with a bridleway opposite. Turn LEFT along the bridleway and descend alongside a small streamlet to a ford and footbridge crossing a more substantial brook. Go through the gate and follow the bridleway to Cross Keys cottage – *which used to be a sheep drovers' inn.*

2 After passing across the front of the cottage, follow the bridleway as it turns RIGHT up the hill. You will pass through an area of open access and then through a field gate into open fields. Keep the fence line to your right until you pass round a field gate doing absolutely nothing and then, after about 20 yards, pass through a second field gate actually doing something. After passing through a further two gates, follow the bridleway as it veers sharp LEFT along the fence. *A glance to your right will enable you to view the radio masts, which this route circumnavigates for much of its length.* As you reach the fence and bridleway crossing your route from left to right, turn RIGHT

towards the radio masts, keeping the fence on your left. You will pass close to the masts and then near to a third mast as you pass through a field gate. Follow the bridleway as it swings off RIGHT down the hill until you reach field gate in the fence.

3 Do not go through the gate but turn RIGHT along the fence and then bear off diagonally RIGHT to the hunting wicket gate in the fence running along the valley bottom. (*Ignore the new metal wicket gate on your left, although it exits onto the track you will soon join, there is no public right of way through it*). After passing through the hunting wicket gate gate, follow the track diagonally to your LEFT until you exit through a field gate onto a substantial track. Turn RIGHT along the track and descend, crossing a stream and turn right again past some sheep pens. Turn RIGHT at the junction and continue to descend until you pass a disused quarry on your left after which the track becomes a tarmac road. Stay on the road, through the gate and follow it back down to the village and to your start point.

About the author and contributors

Richard Dix

Richard was born in the Welsh Marches and has walked extensively in the Welsh uplands as well as, more recently, being involved in the Llanidloes Countryside Access project. This involved identifying, re-establishing, refurbishing and publicising circular routes around the town of Llanidloes and its surrounding villages in order to encourage and facilitate access by both local people and visitors to this beautiful part of Wales. All the routes in this book were born of this process.

Simon Whalley

Simon is a freelance journalist who contributes walking articles for various countryside and walking publications.

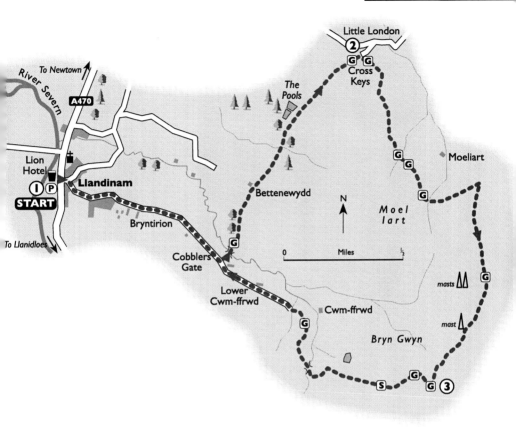

LLANGURIG, MARSH'S POOL AND GLYN BROCHAN

DESCRIPTION A scenic walk of about 6 miles that offers a variety of terrain but with a fairly wet and rough stage at about two thirds of the way round that can be quite testing even in relatively dry weather.

START The Bluebell Inn, Llangurig, (SN 908899).

DIRECTIONS Take the A470 South from Llanidloes and continue for about 5 miles to the junction with the A44, signposted to Llangurig and Aberystwyth. As you drive through Llangurig you will see the Bluebell Inn on your right. Turn RIGHT immediately before the inn and then LEFT into the car park.

I Walk out of the car park and turn LEFT up the hill for about half a mile. Turn RIGHT along the drive to Pen Hyle Mawr farm, signed with a bridleway arrow. On reaching the farm, go into the yard and bear LEFT, out through the gate, and follow the way marks up the hill to Marsh's Pool. Walk down the short lane, keeping the pool to your right, until you reach Glan y Rhyd cottage where there are excellent views around the pool, which can also be circled using footpaths and bridleways should you have the time and energy.

2 Leave the pool, along the track passing behind the cottage, via the wicket gate and follow the bridleway signs AHEAD, up the hill, keeping the fence to your left until you reach the gate and stile into the coniferous wood. Follow the track into the wood and, after about 300 yards or so, look out for the point where the track bears off to the right but there is a small path leading off to your LEFT. Take this path and continue to the field gate. On leaving the wood, keep the fence to your left but skirt to the right to

avoid a patch of gorse and then drop back to your left to pass through a gate AHEAD of you along a wooded, rather wet track, until you emerge, once more, into open fields. As you follow the bridleway up the hill, keep the fence to your left until you reach a gateway on your LEFT bearing a Footpath way mark.

3 Go through the gate and walk up over the hill, keeping the fence to your right. There are good views over Llanidloes to your right as you descend to The Farm. On reaching The Farm, go into the yard and then bear LEFT in front of the house and then AHEAD through the field gate. Follow the way marks down the hill and through a small wood, past the ruined cottage and then cross the stream over a footbridge, continue AHEAD, up the hill and through two gates onto the tarmac road. Turn RIGHT along the road and after about 120 yards or so, turn LEFT to Upper Glynbrochan farm. When you reach the yard in front of the house, bear RIGHT where you will come to a gate on your LEFT marked as a bridleway. *Do not take the gate ahead marked as a footpath.* Go through the gate and follow the well marked track, through a fairly wet patch, past Pen y Maes farm and on, out over open fields, keeping the fence to your left, to Rhyd yr Orfa where the track joins another bridleway passing from right to left.

4 Turn LEFT along the new track and follow the way marks up the hill. As you cross the summit you will have to cross a very wet and muddy patch that can be avoided somewhat by moving to your right and crossing farther up. Rejoin the track and go through the field gate AHEAD of you. If you look diagonally right, you will see the gate you will need to go through next. However, to avoid the extremely wet and rough patch on your route, it is best to keep the fence on your RIGHT and to follow it around to the gate rather than walk straight across. After passing through the gate, cut across the LEFT hand corner of the field to the next gate and then bear diagonally RIGHT, through the gate and then go AHEAD and follow the way marked track down, across the fields to Hir

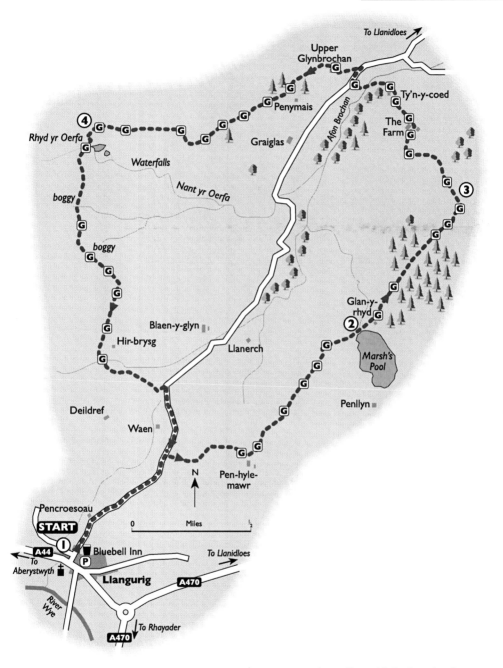

Brysg. Join the well established track taking you to the road and then bear RIGHT, back down to Llangurig and your start point.

DEILDRE FAWR, LLWYN DERW AND BRITHDIR

DESCRIPTION An interesting walk of about 6 miles (or 2½ miles for the shorter alternative), passing down through old mine workings in a deep, wooded valley, then over open fields and along part of the Severn Way before climbing gently back out past a local sculpture studio and an old sheep wash to the start.

START Picnic area, Clywedog, (SN 904872).

DIRECTIONS From Llanidloes drive along Long Bridge Street to the mini-roundabout and turn LEFT over the bridge and immediately LEFT again along the B4518 sign posted to Llyn Clywedog. Stay on this road for about 2 miles before turning LEFT again for Llyn Clywedog. You will reach the dam after about 1½ miles. Drive past the viewing area and continue for almost half a mile to where the road bears left and you come to a picnic area on your right, close to two lay-bys. This is your start point.

I Leave the picnic area and turn RIGHT along the road for about 150 yards, when you will come to the farm drive to Deildre Fawr on your left. Go over the cattle grid and down the drive and, where the track bears right into the farm, go through the field gate AHEAD of you and then bear LEFT across the field, aiming for Penwar hill on the other side of the valley. Go through the gate and follow the path down through the trees. As the path descends along a stream to your left, you might notice the old mine workings on the far side of the narrow valley. Continue, keeping the stream on your left, down through a gate until you reach the huts belonging to a shooting club. Turn RIGHT here, through a wicket gate, and cross the Nant Gwestyn over a footbridge just below the falls. Go up the track, through the gate for about 100 yards until you see an old quarry in front of you. At this point, turn RIGHT

into the field and up the valley, picking up the track that will take you out onto the tarmac road. (*At this point, you may reduce the length of your walk to about 2½ miles by turning right along the road and continuing as at* **4** *below*).

2 Turn LEFT along the road for about 250 yards, over a cattle grid, and then for about another 150 yards when you will come to three field gates, side by side on your RIGHT. Go through the LEFT hand gate and keep the fence to your right all the way as you go through two more gates over open fields and pick up the track taking you on down the hill to Llwyn Derw. Go straight AHEAD along the farm track to the tarmac road below.

3 Turn RIGHT along the Severn Way, bearing RIGHT where the road forks. Continue along the road for just over 1½ miles. You may see the burgeoning River Severn below you, to your left as you walk along the road. After crossing a cattle grid, if you look up to your right, you should see the farm track joining you from behind, almost parallel with the road. At it's junction with the road, some 150 yards farther on, turn RIGHT, up along the track to Brithdir, a sculpture studio with several items on display to view as you pass by, and then continue AHEAD, keeping the buildings to your right, and follow the track out to the tarmac road beyond.

4 Turn LEFT along the road for just under a quarter of a mile until the road drops down to cross the Nant Gwestyn. Notice the old sheep wash to your right before going through the road gate and, ignoring the road that bears left up the hill, continuing AHEAD along the track back to Deildre Fawr. This road offers excellent views down the Nant Gwestyn valley and over to the wind farm above Llandinam in the distance. On reaching the farm, go straight through the buildings before following the track off to your LEFT, back out to the tarmac road along which you turn RIGHT and back to your start point.

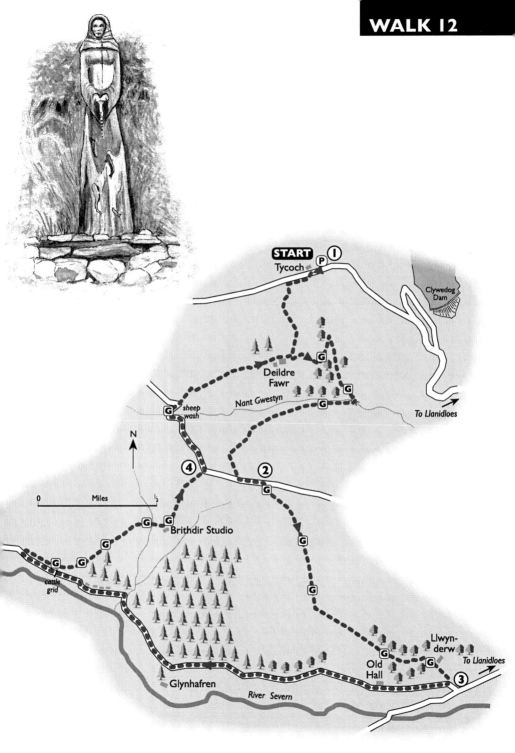

START
Tycoch
P
1
Clywedog Dam
Deildre Fawr
G
G
sheep wash
G
Nant Gwestyn
G
To Llanidloes
N
4
2
G
0   Miles   ½
G
G
Brithdir Studio
G
G
cattle grid
G
Old Hall
G
Llwyn-derw
G
To Llanidloes
3
Glynhafren
River Severn

TREFEGLWYS AND LLYN EBYR

DESCRIPTION A walk of approximately 10 miles, taking in views of the Trannon and Severn valleys and passing alongside Llyn Ebyr through old, deciduous woodland.

START The Red Lion pub, Trefeglwys, (SN 971908).

DIRECTIONS From Llanidloes, take the B4569 North to Trefeglwys. The Red Lion will be found on the far side of the village on your left.

I From the Red Lion car park, turn LEFT and walk north, through the village and take the first turn RIGHT after the primary school. Continue along this road as it passes through a small estate, enters open countryside and reaches the bridge over the river Trannon. After crossing the bridge, ignore the gateway to your right signposted Pen y Wern and, instead, go through the field gate AHEAD and walk across the middle of the field to a footbridge crossing a broad ditch. After crossing the bridge, look for the stile diagonally to your LEFT, cross the stile and go through the field gate AHEAD, following the fence around the white house (Wern), keeping it to your right, until you come to the concrete drive. Turn LEFT along the drive, cross the cattle grid and turn RIGHT, keeping the hedge to your right until you reach and cross the footbridge over the Cerist. (*This footbridge was missing at the time of writing and was due to be replaced. If it is not in position when you reach the river, simply turn LEFT along the Cerist to the next bridge, marked with a 10mph limit, cross it and immediately turn RIGHT through the field gate and follow the Cerist back to the original bridge site at point 2).*

2 Turn RIGHT and continue along the Cerist until you reach a field gate next to a farm bridge. Go through the gate and turn LEFT between the two fences. As you emerge into the open field, walk up towards the top RIGHT hand corner of the field into Pant Farm. Walk through the farm and, at the farmhouse, turn RIGHT along the tarmac road. After about 500 yards you will pass a tarmac lane joining you from your left and about 50 yards past the lane you will note a bridleway gateway set back from the road on your left.

3 Go LEFT through the gate and follow the track through the trees, on through a field gate and, keeping the fence line to your left, proceed through a further gate into open fields and on to Cylch Farm. Walk through the farm buildings and follow the track down, past the bungalow to the tarmac road. [*Alternatively, follow the slightly shorter permissive bridleway, marked with green arrows, to rejoin the described route at point 4*]. On reaching the road, turn LEFT and continue to Bwlch y Llyn farm. Go through the farm gate to your front and, keeping the buildings to your right, pass through another gate out of the farm. Follow the track to the RIGHT between an old shed on your left and a fence on your right. After about 50 yards take the lower path to your RIGHT into the trees and alongside Llyn Ebyr. Walk through this deciduous woodland and, ignoring the track turning up the hill to your left, pass through the gate AHEAD of you into a coniferous wood. On emerging from the wood into open fields, follow the track as it climbs up the slope to your LEFT and away from the lake.

24

Follow the track around the side of the hill and through a field gate at the top, right hand corner, to Pen y Castell farm.

4 Do not enter the farm but, instead where you join the main farm track, turn

village of Llandinam. Continue, keeping the hedge to your left, through another gate and, passing a stone water trough on your left, pass through the RIGHT hand gate of the two in front of you. Follow the hedge for about 150 yards as it then curves off LEFT up and through a gate. Continue with the hedge on your left until you reach a belt of small trees. ‡ Turn RIGHT in front of the trees and follow them down until you pick up the track once as it curves off RIGHT and

Bodaloch
Hall

N

Wern

Afon Cerist

②

Ty'n-y-celyn

Red House

Earthworks

Pant

Brynbedw

⑤

0   Miles   ½

Motte &
Bailey

Pen-y-castell
Wood

G ⇠ ④

through a field gate hanging on living oak tree. Continue along the track, bearing slightly LEFT towards the woodland fence. Turn LEFT along the fence and after a short distance go through the gate AHEAD into the wood and bear right along the track, taking the right fork a little further in until you reach the gate leading out of the wood into open fields.

5 Keeping the fence line to your left, follow the track until you reach a small stand of birch trees, where you go through the gate AHEAD and descend, keeping to your left around the shoulder of the slope. You will soon come in sight of a small wooden cottage called Cwm y Garth. Keep to the left of the cottage and then follow the track down past Trewythen Fach to the tarmac road, at which point, turn left and follow the road some two miles back to the Red Lion.

LEFT along the track, away from the farm and on through the field gate AHEAD of you into open fields once more. On your right you may enjoy extensive views across the Severn Valley to the wind turbines along Yr Allt Gethin and Waun Debarthog above the

LLANGURIG, GLAN FEDWEN AND THE ELAN VALLEY

DESCRIPTION A more challenging walk of about 10½ miles, taking in fields, forest and moorland with some fairly steep slopes over rough ground. There is an opportunity, part way round, to take a short cut and reduce the walking distance to just over 6 miles.
START The Bluebell Inn, Llangurig, (SN 908899).
DIRECTIONS As **Walk 8**.

I Turn RIGHT out of the car park and then LEFT along the main road. Between the Post Office and Craft Shop, turn RIGHT along the road and cross the River Wye. At this point you join the Wye Valley Walk for a little way. Bear RIGHT at the fork and, after about 250 yards, go through the gateway on your RIGHT marked as a bridleway. Follow the track as it zigzags up the side of the hill on your left and, on the ridge, joins another track coming in from your left. Turn RIGHT along this track and continue along the ridge for almost a mile, until you reach a gateway next to some sheep pens.

2 The bridleway divides at this point and you should bear LEFT here to follow the track around and along the side of the hill. Although faint at first, the track becomes more visible a little farther on. Follow the track to a wicket gate in the forestry fence and, passing through the gate, walk AHEAD, keeping the tree line to your right, until you reach a broad forestry track crossing from right to left. (*At this point you may reduce the overall length of your walk to about 6 miles by turning right here, going directly to point 6 and following the*

return directions from there).

3 Turn LEFT along the broad track for about 100 yards and then, just past a fire beating station, turn RIGHT along a narrower track climbing through the trees and follow it to a wicket gate at the forest edge. Go through the gate and walk AHEAD, along the ridge of the hill as it slowly descends. Before the last, steeper slope to the valley floor, bear LEFT and go through the gate you will see in the fence across your front. (*The ground here is quite rough and wet and you need to look out for some of the deeper holes.*) After passing through the gate, bear RIGHT to cross the stream and then locate the Rain Gauge to ensure you are in the right location. With the stream behind you, climb the side of the hill to your front until you are some 50 yards or so away from the

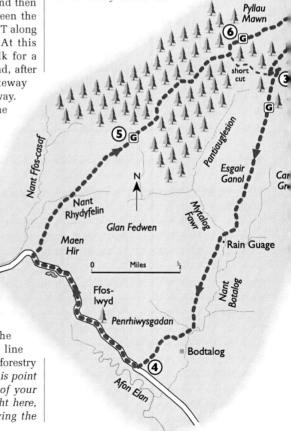

Pyllau Mawn

short cut

Pantiaugiesion

Esgair Ganol

Car Gr

N

Nant Ffos-casaf

Mynalog Fawr

Nant Rhydyfelin

Glan Fedwen

Maen Hir

Rain Guage

0   Miles   ½

Ffos-lwyd

Nant Botalog

Penrhiwysgadan

Bodtalog

Afon Elan

26

stream, and then turn LEFT along the hillside and down the valley, keeping the stream to your left, to Bodtalog Farm. When you reach the farm fence, turn RIGHT along the fence line then follow it as it curves LEFT and then AHEAD down to the finger post and the tarmac road.

5 Ignore the track that appears to go up the hill to your left and walk AHEAD, into the gap through the trees. The track here is quite narrow in places and often seems to peter out. Do not be tempted to follow more distinct gaps in the trees to your left or right, but continue along the line the track until you can see a broad forestry track slightly above you on your left, which your own track will meet. Turn RIGHT along the broad track. After 150 yards or so you will note another track joining you from your right and, farther on still, you will come to a track curving off to your left, by a fire beating station. (You are now at point **6** and, if you were to continue ahead, you would return to point **3** after about 300 yards)

6 Turn LEFT here and, after about 50 yards or so, turn RIGHT along a trail through the trees and follow it for about 100 yards to a wicket gate. Go through the gate out onto the hill and follow the track as it bears RIGHT up onto the ridgeline. Once on the top of the ridge, bear LEFT along the centre of the ridge and follow it down and back to the sheep pens and gate at point **2**. As you descend you will have excellent views of the wind farms at Carno to your left, Llandinam ahead of you and Bryn Titli to your right. From point **2**, retrace your route back down to the tarmac road and turn LEFT to go back to Llangurig and your start point.

4 You are now in the upper Elan Valley. Turn RIGHT along the road for about a mile. You will pass a stand of trees on your right at about the half way point, and then a pool down to your left before you turn RIGHT at the finger post about 300 yards beyond. The bridleway is easy to follow up to and along the ridge of the hill until, after about a mile, you come to a wicket gate in the forestry fence line with a short stretch of open field before you enter the trees.

DYLIFE, TWYMYN VALLEY AND PENTRE CILCWM

DESCRIPTION A very scenic and, in parts, spectacular walk along the side of and then climbing out of, a glaciated valley having SSSI designation. The walk is about 6 miles long and very steep at one point as you climb out of the head of the valley. The views are impressive and include streams cascading down the steep valley sides. *This walk should NOT be attempted after heavy rain or when the river is in spate.*

START Roadside parking below the Star Inn at Dylife, (SN 861940).

DIRECTIONS From Llanidloes, take the B4518, signposted for Llyn Clywedog and Staylittle. Stay on the road for about 8 miles until you reach Staylittle and then continue for a further 1¾ miles or so before turning LEFT for Dylife. After about half a mile you will pass a finger post on your right (to which you will return) and then a viewpoint, also on your right. About three quarters of a mile past the viewpoint you will note the remains of old mine workings on your right. Turn RIGHT just past the workings and park on some of the open ground at the side of the road.

I Walk back down the road, and pause at the viewpoint where there is an information board and excellent views down the valley. Continue down the road and turn LEFT at the finger post. The track is well defined and climbs initially, before following the ridgeline alongside the valley. You will pass through four gates as you slowly descend with magnificent views of the valley and Afon Twymwn to your left. Near the head of the valley, on the opposite side, you may note a cluster of tepee type dwellings. *This is a site used for much of the year by groups wishing to experience alternative lifestyles and you will pass through the settlement later as you approach the climb out of the*

valley. Continue on to the point where a track drops down the hill to your left and pause.

2 At this point look across the valley and to your right to the farm, Cilcwm Fawr, below you. To avoid confusion later, you should note the fence on the hillside along the back of the farm, along which the path goes rather than going through the farm itself. Descend along the track dropping down to your LEFT to its link with the tarmac drive. Follow the drive towards Cilcwm Fawr and, just before the drive bears left in front of the farmhouse, look out for and follow the footpath signs taking you RIGHT, through a concrete yard and then bear LEFT along the fence as it climbs the hill along the fence behind the buildings. The path passes through a gate before dropping down to your LEFT to the river. Turn RIGHT alongside the river, keeping it to your left, and follow the path along the bottom of the ridge where the route is considerably drier then further out into the valley. The path continues through four gates and then crosses over the river some 100 yards or so farther on. Keep the river to your right now as you follow the bends and re-cross it, passing through field gate on the far side and walking AHEAD towards the settlement.

3 After about 100 yards, look out for the way marks and follow them LEFT, up the hill and follow the track as it zigzags it's way out of the head of the valley. This section is very steep and you should take advantage of many pauses to admire the view. At the top follow the path as it bears diagonally right to the stile. Climb over the stile into the field and continue AHEAD, keeping the fence line on your right, and follow the fence down to the small river, Nant Bryn Moel, along which you turn LEFT to the bridge. Cross the bridge and go through the gate, following well-defined track up the slope and through the gate into the field where you continue AHEAD and then go through the gate and onto the tarmac drive by the house. Follow the drive and bear RIGHT at the fork to the Star Inn. You may, of course pause here for refreshment but, no doubt, the more hardy souls will continue the 200 yards or so back to their vehicles at the start point.

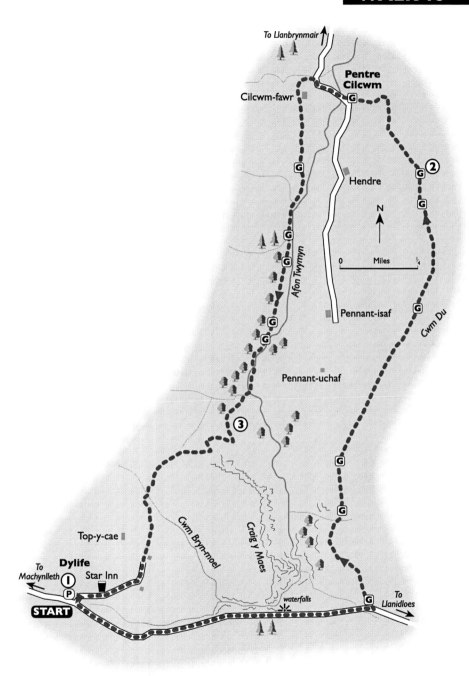

To Llanbrynmair

Pentre Cilcwm

Cilcwm-fawr

Hendre

N

0 ____ Miles ____ ¼

Afon Twymyn

Pennant-isaf

Cwm Du

Pennant-uchaf

③

Cwm Bryn-moel

Craig y Maes

Top-y-cae

Dylife

To Machynlleth

Star Inn

waterfalls

To Llanidloes

START

②

29

MOELFRE

DESCRIPTION A relatively short walk of about 3½ miles but with pretty views over the Newchapel valley, broadening out as you climb to afford excellent views over the Severn Valley itself. The walk is fairly steep to the summit of Moelfre but this is then followed by a more leisurely descent and some more level walking.

START Lane entrance just beyond a bungalow near Newchapel, (SO 996843).

DIRECTIONS From Llanidloes take the B4518 to the A470 and turn LEFT. After about 2½ miles take the RIGHT turn signposted to Newchapel and then take the RIGHT fork after about half a mile. After about 200 yards you will come to a bungalow on your left with the lane entrance start to your walk immediately after. Drive past the entrance for a few yards to where the road widens to a lay-by where there is space to park your car.

I Walk back towards the bungalow and turn RIGHT into the lane. Continue along the lane as it gradually descends to the stream in the valley bottom. At the ford follow the lane LEFT as it climbs for about 200 yards to Celyn barn. Go through the gate and into the yard, keeping the building to your right. Turn RIGHT behind the barn and follow the lane for just over 100 yards and go through the next gate. Leave the lane at this point and keep to the fence line, bearing LEFT up the field for about 200 yards. Continue to follow the fence as it turns sharp LEFT at this point and then, after a further 100 yards, sharp RIGHT up the hill and pass through a gate out onto the hillside. Climb the hill bearing to the RIGHT of the ridge line until you reach the gate in the fence running from left to right just over the summit.

2 After going through the gate, bear diagonally LEFT over the field until you reach a hardcore track comiing down the hill from your left. Join the track and turn RIGHT down the hill to the bottom fence. Turn LEFT along the inside of the fence and, at the end of the field, cross over two stiles. Within a few yards of the stiles you will reach a junction at which Glyndŵr's Way is signposted off to your right and the bridleway is signposted off to your left. Bear LEFT along the bridleway and follow it as it descends through deciduous woodland. Ignore the apparent fork down to your right and continue along the woodland walk until you reach a field gate. As you go through into the field, follow the track now marked by a series of trees for about another 100 yards before descending diagonally RIGHT to the lower edge of the field. At the fence, turn LEFT and go through the right hand gate of two set in the fence ahead of you, crossing a small stream running along the far side of the fence. Cross this fairly narrow field and go through the next gate into an unimproved boggy field. Cross straight over to the lane ahead of you, leading out of the field onto the tarmac road. Turn LEFT along the road to the T junction at Bryncoch Farm and turn LEFT again for about ¾ mile to the next junction at which you turn LEFT back to your start point.

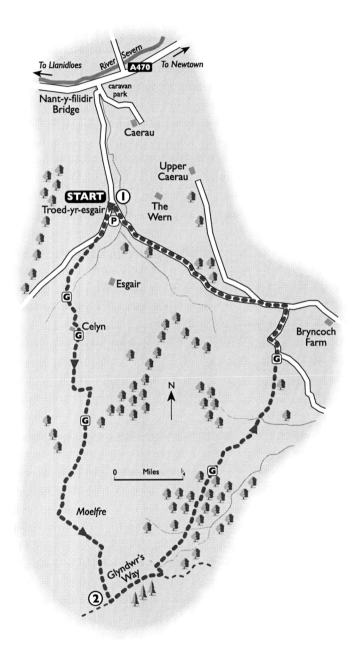

BRYN MAWR AND CWM GWERNOG

DESCRIPTION One of the shorter walks of about 3½ miles, but very rewarding with views opening over Cwm Gwernog and the Trannon valley and with the last half mile or so alongside Nant Cwm Gwernog, a small but busy brook that crosses your route three times within the last 250 yards of your walk. There is a fairly steep climb along the single-track, tarmac road to begin with but, if you take your time, the rewarding scenery is well worth the effort. **START** Llawr y glyn village, (SN 932913).

DIRECTIONS From Llanidloes take the B4569 north for about 4 miles to the village of Trefeglwys and, after passing the garage on a sharp left-hand bent, turn LEFT at the post office and continue for about 2½ miles to the small village of Llawr y glyn. In the village, turn RIGHT and after about 150 yards there is limited parking on a small grassed area by the brook.

I Take the LEFT hand, single track road, signed as a cul-de-sac, which climbs up the hill and continue for just over half a mile until you reach a point where the road rises steeply then drops away as it curves round to Gwernau Farm. You will note a telegraph pole on your right opposite a broad lane entrance way-marked as a bridleway. Turn LEFT along the lane and follow it as it then bears right up the hillside. Go through two gates then turn sharp LEFT to continue following the track as it approaches the gate to a small holding, then swings RIGHT once more up the hill. *The views to your right and behind you along this stretch are particularly impressive and, after your earlier climb, this*

section is certainly worth a more leisurely ramble. After passing through two more gates, the track curves left then right before meeting a third gate adjacent to a corner of Gors Goch wood, where your track is joined by another approaching from your right. You will note that this new track is signed by green and white way-marks as a permissive footpath.

2 Turn RIGHT along this track and, after passing through a gate, follow it as it turns RIGHT down the valley, passing a small pool on your right and a bridge on your left. The track continues down alongside the embryonic Nant Cwmgwernog brook until it reaches the shearing barn at Cwm-llymwynt. Keeping the barn to your left, go through two gates and then follow the track RIGHT for about 150 yards until you reach a shallow ford and gateway. Do not go through the gate but turn LEFT along the track to continue down the valley for about 400 yards, over another shallow ford and through a field gate. After a further 200 yards or so look out for the stile next to a gateway on your LEFT where the permissive path leaves the track. Cross the stile and go AHEAD down the field to the wicket gate and, passing through it, continue AHEAD, keeping the fence line to your right until you descend to a farm track. Follow this track down the hill until you reach the gate to Cwm-gwernog Farm. Go AHEAD through the gate and down through the farm buildings, exiting through the gate next to the farmhouse. Walk out along the farm driveway with the Nant Cwmgwernog brook on your right. This is a picturesque valley walk which comes to a particularly satisfying conclusion as you ford the brook three times before returning to your start point.

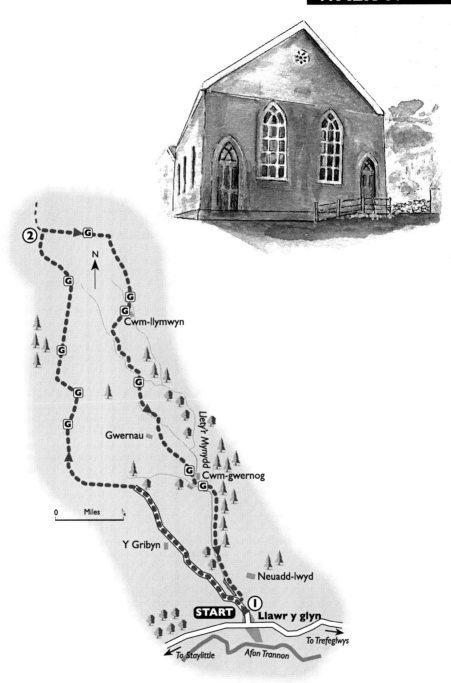

Cwm-llymwyn

N

2

Gwernau

Llety'r Mynydd

Cwm-gwernog

0   Miles   ¼

Y Gribyn

Neuadd-lwyd

START   1   Llawr y glyn

To Staylittle   Afon Trannon   To Trefeglwys

BRYN MAWR, GORS GOCH AND WAUN

DESCRIPTION This walk takes in stage one of the previous walk and then goes on through Gors Goch forest, out onto Waun moor and returns via Mawnog Bryn-glas. The first part of the forest section can be difficult and wet underfoot, as can parts of the moorland, but the walker is well rewarded by gorgeous views over the Trannon valley. The total distance is just less than 6 miles.

START Llawr y glyn village, (SN 932913).

DIRECTIONS From Llanidloes take the B4569 north for about 4 miles to the village of Trefeglwys and, after passing the garage on a sharp left-hand bent, turn LEFT at the post office and continue for about 2½ miles to the small village of Llawr y glyn. In the village, turn RIGHT and after about 150 yards there is limited parking on a small grassed area by the brook.

I Take the LEFT hand, single track road, signed as a cul-de-sac, which climbs up the hill and continue for just over half a mile until you reach a point where the road rises steeply then drops away as it curves round to Gwernau Farm. You will note a telegraph pole on your right opposite a broad lane entrance way-marked as a bridleway. Turn LEFT along the lane and follow it as it then bears right up the hillside. Go through two gates then turn sharp LEFT to continue following the track as it approaches the gate to a small holding, then swings RIGHT once more up the hill. *The views to your right and behind you along this stretch are particularly impressive and, after your earlier climb, this section is certainly worth a more leisurely ramble.* After passing through two more gates, the track curves left then right before

meeting a third gate adjacent to a corner of Gors Goch wood, where your track is joined by another approaching from your right.

2 Continue AHEAD through the gate and follow the track to the wicket gate, going through the gate into Gors Goch wood. The going here can be quite wet and rough underfoot. Follow the way-marked bridleway through the wood until you reach the hard-core topped forestry track across your front. *(Be careful at this point as this track is often used by a local car rally training school).* Cross the track and continue to follow the way marks the short distance to the wicket gate in the forest fence. On leaving the forest take the path across the moor which first takes you AHEAD to the cairn on the summit then bears gently downhill and to your RIGHT until it meets the far corner of the forest. At the corner, go through the wicket gate and then walk AHEAD keeping the forest fence to your right for about 500 yards until you reach another wicket gate taking you back into Gors Goch.

3 Go through the wicket gate and walk AHEAD for about 150 yards to the hardcore topped forestry track and then continue AHEAD, past a small pool on your left, to the field gate taking you out of the wood onto open fields. Follow the track on through two gates and, at the second gate, walk AHEAD across the field then turn RIGHT along the fence. Ignore the gateway you pass after a few yards and, keeping the fence to your left, go through the gate in the corner of the field. *As the view ahead of you opens up, look to your right, across the valley to the route you took initially when climbing to the forest on Bryn Mawr.* Follow the track on down Banc y Neuadd past a wood to your right, through a further gate and down into Neuadd-lwyd farm where you go through the buildings, bear LEFT in front of the farmhouse and then RIGHT, along the drive and back to your start point.

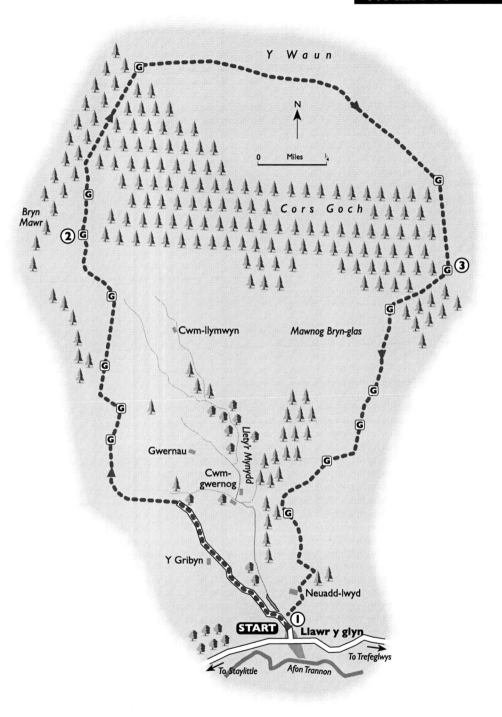

Y Waun

N

0   Miles   ¼

Bryn
Mawr

② G

G

Cors Goch

③

G

Cwm-llymwyn   Mawnog Bryn-glas

G

G

G

G

G

Gwernau

Llety'r Mynydd

Cwm-
gwernog

G

Y Gribyn

G

Neuadd-lwyd

START ① Llawr y glyn

To Trefeglwys

To Staylittle   Afon Trannon

LLAWR Y GLYN AND BRYN CRUGOG

DESCRIPTION A walk of about 4 miles around Bryn Crugog hill, with a fairly steep climb out of Neuadd-lwyd farm, rewarded by extensive views over the Trannon valley. The going underfoot is good for almost all the distance and there is an alternative return route offering a less steep descent into Geseilfa farm.

START Llawr y glyn village, (SN 932913).

DIRECTIONS From Llanidloes take the B4569 north for about 4 miles to the village of Trefeglwys and, after passing the garage on a sharp left-hand bent, turn LEFT at the post office and continue for about 2½ miles to the small village of Llawr y glyn. In the village, turn RIGHT and after about 150 yards there is limited parking on a small grassed area by the brook

1 Cross the bridge over the Nant Cwmgwernog brook and walk AHEAD, up the drive to Neuadd-lwydd farm. Turn LEFT into the yard then RIGHT through the buildings and exit along the track way-marked as a bridleway. Walk along the track as it climbs the hill and go through a gate at the beginning of some woodland to your left, after which the climb becomes quite steep, affording ample opportunity to pause and admire the views back over the Trannon valley as you gain your second wind. After passing through a second gate and keeping the fence to your right, walk AHEAD until you pass a gateway on your right and reach the point where the bridleway leaves the fence line. Turn LEFT along this somewhat fainter track, crossing the field to the gate into the next field, through which you walk directly

AHEAD, through yet another gate and along the bottom of a slope and fence line on your right, until you reach the gate into Gors Goch wood. Walk along the hard-core forestry track for about 200 yards, passing a small pool on your right, until you reach a finger post directing you AHEAD, off the track and to a wicket gate in the forest fence some 150 yards in front of you.

2 Go through the gate and continue AHEAD over some rough ground for about 200 yards after which you will descend to a hard-core track crossing the Waun moor. Turn RIGHT along the track and go through the gate onto the tarmac road. Turn RIGHT along the road and enjoy the views ahead as you as you walk down the road for 700 yards or so until you reach a tarmac lane joining you from your left. About 120 yards past the lane, turn RIGHT through a way-marked field gate* and then through a second gate immediately to your LEFT. Walk ahead through the middle of the field, keeping to the right of the area of marsh grass, for about 300 yards when you will come to a field gate across a small bridge. Go through the gate and turn immediately LEFT along the fence and then down the fairly steep slope to the gate into the farm lane. Go through the gate and then turn LEFT then RIGHT down the lane and follow the lane down through a further gate into Geseilfa farm. Keeping the buildings to your left, continue down the track to the tarmac road along which you turn RIGHT and walk the half mile or so back to your start point.

Should you wish to avoid the fairly steep drop down a grassy slope along this section, you may walk about a quarter of a mile further along the road to a sharp left-hand bend and turn RIGHT along the farm lane way-marked as a permissive path that will take you down to Geseilfa farm less steeply.

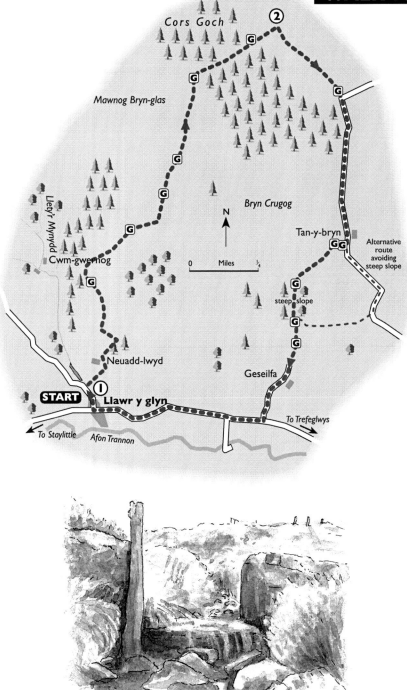

Cors Goch

Mawnog Bryn-glas

Llety'r Mynydd

Cwm-gwernog

Bryn Crugog

N

0   Miles   ¼

Tan-y-bryn

Alternative route avoiding steep slope

steep slope

Neuadd-lwyd

Geseilfa

START ① Llawr y glyn

To Staylittle   Afon Trannon

To Trefeglwys

FOEL GOCH
& BRYN MAWR

DESCRIPTION A quite challenging walk of just over 5 miles with terrain varying from cultivated fields to unimproved lowland including a short section of forestry.

START Lay-By close to Bwlch y garreg, (SN 935798).

DIRECTIONS From Llanidloes take the A470 south for about 3½ miles and look out for the 400-yard stretch of woodland on your right and the stream on your left. Towards the end of the woodland, on a significant right hand bend, turn LEFT along a minor road, passing the lane to Bwlch y Garreg farm on your left almost immediately and continue for a further 400 yards or so until you see the wicket gate at the start of your walk on your RIGHT. There is limited parking space at various points where the road widens.

I Go through the gate and walk up the slope over the rough terrain keeping the fence to your right and a ditch to your left until you reach the second wicket gate. If you look ahead up the hill at this point, you may see your next gate 250 yards ahead of you, in the fence to your right. Bear diagonally LEFT up the hill for some 200 yards then RIGHT towards the gate. Go AHEAD through the gate and keep the fence to your right as you go to and through the next gate, bearing LEFT along the track through the trees. As you leave the trees, follow the track over the open field to the next gate and then bear diagonally LEFT across the next field for about 250 yards to the crest of the ridge. At this point, turn LEFT towards the gate near the corner of the forest and, after going through the gate, follow the forest fence to where it bends RIGHT and, after a further 150 yards, go through the gate into the forest. Follow the track down through the trees and bear LEFT at the bottom to the wicket gate in the fence.

2 Leaving the forest, bear slightly RIGHT down to the corner of the field and go AHEAD through the gate onto a track. After about 100 yards, go through the field gate on your RIGHT, then bear diagonally LEFT to the far fence, turning LEFT along the fence and through the wicket gate in the corner. From the gate, bear right around the shoulder of the hill, keeping about 25 yards above the unimproved wetland below you on your right, past a Tir Gofal marker on your right, for about 600 yards. As the valley flattens ahead of you, look for the area of forestry over to your left with a wicket gate about 200 yards in from the right hand corner. *You cannot walk directly to the gate because of deep stream crossing in front of it.* Instead aim for the field gate in the fence about 150 yards to the RIGHT of the plantation, indicated by the marker post, until you cross the bridge over the stream, then turn LEFT along the far bank of the stream to the wicket gate. Go through the gate into the plantation and, keeping the fence to your right, make your way around and up through the trees until you reach a more substantial track and bridleway junction. (*To avoid the quite difficult conditions underfoot in the trees, the landowner has permitted you to cross the bridge and then go through the gate immediately AHEAD of you into the field, after which you turn LEFT along the fence outside the plantation and continue over a further bridge, up the field until you meet the bridleway coming into the plantation from your right at the above junction*). Continue AHEAD along the track to where it passes onto a tarmac surfaced road that meanders down the hill to the road junction on the valley floor.

3 Pass two possible right turns and, after about 200 yards, look out for and walk along a lane on your RIGHT marked by a bridleway marker on the telegraph pole at the entrance. (*Those walkers feeling tired at this point may save themselves a climb and about ¾ mile by simply continuing along the road back to their vehicle*). Go through the farm gate and through the buildings, passing to the left of the house. Exit the farm through a further gate and follow the track through two more gates to its junction with

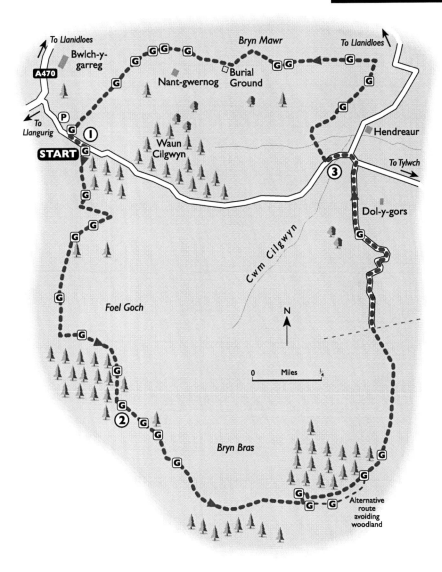

a more substantial track by a cattle grid. Turn LEFT along the track and, keeping the fence to your right follow it on through open fields and through a sheep enclosure and past a small, disused quarry. On passing the quarry go through the gate into the field and bear diagonally LEFT to the bottom corner of the field exiting through the gate in the RIGHT hand fence. Keeping the fence to your left, you will pass almost immediately a walled Quaker burial ground – *dating from the 18th century.* Go through a further two fields until you come to two gates side by side. Go through the RIGHT hand gate and then follow the track on down the hill until you reach the tarmac road below and turn LEFT to return to your vehicle.

PRONUNCIATION

These basic points should help non-Welsh speakers

Welsh	English equivalent
c	always hard, as in cat
ch	as on the Scottish word loch
dd	as th in then
f	as v in vocal
ff	as f
g	always hard as in got
ll	no real equivalent. It is like 'th' in then, but with an 'L' sound added to it, giving 'thlan' for the pronunciation of the Welsh 'Llan'.

In Welsh the accent usually falls on the last-but-one syllable of a word.

KEY TO THE MAPS

▬▬▬	Main road
▬▬	Minor road
●►►	Walk route and direction
①	Walk instruction
– – –	Path
∿	River/stream
Ⓖ	Gate
Ⓢ	Stile
△	Summit
♣♠	Woods
▮	Pub
Ⓟ	Parking

THE COUNTRYSIDE CODE

- Be safe – plan ahead and follow any signs
- Leave gates and property as you find them
- Protect plants and animals, and take your litter home
- Keep dogs under close control
- Consider other people

The CroW Act 2000, implemented throughout Wales in May 2005, introduced new legal rights of access for walkers to designated open country, predominantly mountain, moor, heath or down, plus all registered common land (see CCW's leaflet 'New Access to the Countryside in Wales' available from TICs). This access can be subject to restrictions and closure for land management or safety reasons for up to 28 days a year.

The following web site operated by Countryside Council for Wales will provide updated information on any closures.

www.ccw.gov.uk/countrysideaccesswales

Published by
Kittiwake
3 Glantwymyn Village Workshops, Glantwymyn, Machynlleth, Montgomeryshire SY20 8LY

© Text & map research: Richard Dix 2006
© Maps & illustrations: Kittiwake 2006
Drawings by Morag Perrott

Cover photos: *Main – Bryntail Mine: Simon Whalley. Inset – Llanidloes Market Hall: Llani Limited.*

Printed by MWL, Pontypool.

ISBN: **1 902302 44 3**